THE MINNESOTA VIKINGS

Sloan MacRae

PowerKiDS press

New York

Published in 2011 by The Rosen Publishing Group, Inc.
29 East 21st Street, New York, NY 10010

First Edition

Editors: Sara Antill and Amelie von Zumbusch
Book Design: Greg Tucker
Layout Design: Julio Gil

Photo Credits: Cover (Fran Tarkenton), p. 7 Andy Hayt/Getty Images; cover (Adrian Peterson) p. 21 Ronald Martinez/Getty Images; cover (Cris Carter), p. 17 Allen Kee/Getty Images; cover (background) Scott Boehm/Getty Images; pp. 5, 11, 22 (top) Focus On Sport/Getty Images; p. 9 Hunter Martin/ Getty Images; p. 13 Vernon Biever/Getty Images; p. 15 Ronald C. Modra/Getty Images; p. 19 Chris Graythen/Getty Images; p. 22 (bottom) Chris McGrath/Getty Images.

Library of Congress Cataloging-in-Publication Data

MacRae, Sloan.
 The Minnesota Vikings / by Sloan MacRae. — 1st ed.
     p. cm. — (America's greatest teams)
 Includes index.
 ISBN 978-1-4488-3168-5 (library binding) — ISBN 978-1-4488-3174-6 (pbk.) —
 ISBN 978-1-4488-3175-3 (6-pack)
 1. Minnesota Vikings (Football team)—History—Juvenile literature. I. Title.
 GV956.M5M33 2011
 796.332'6409776579—dc22
                                              2010039419

Manufactured in the United States of America

CPSIA Compliance Information: Batch #WW11PK: For Further Information contact Rosen Publishing, New York, New York at 1-800-237-9932

CONTENTS

UNLUCKY IN THE SUPER BOWL

Football fans often believe that the best football teams win the most **Super Bowls**. This is not always the case. The Super Bowl is the biggest game of the year for the National Football **League**, or the NFL. Only the best team from each **conference** gets to play in the Super Bowl. Some teams have never even played in one.

The Minnesota Vikings have reached more Super Bowls than most NFL teams. However, they have not yet won one. This does not make them a bad team. The Vikings have still had many winning seasons. They are one of the greatest teams in NFL history.

In this picture, Vikings defensive back Nate Wright tries to stop Larry Csonka of the Miami Dolphins during the Vikings' second Super Bowl.

WHAT'S A VIKING?

The Vikings football team is based in Minnesota's Minneapolis-St. Paul area. The cities of Minneapolis and St. Paul, Minnesota, are very close together. They are often called the Twin Cities.

The team gets its name from a group of tough fighters called Vikings. These Vikings lived hundreds of years ago. They were from Scandinavia but traveled widely. Many settlers from Scandinavia moved to Minnesota in the mid-1800s. This is why the Vikings is such a good name for a tough Minnesota football team.

The Vikings' colors are purple, gold, and white. Their **logo** shows what a real Viking may have looked like.

Here you can see the horn shape on quarterback Fran Tarkenton's helmet. The Vikings from history may have worn real horns on their helmets.

SKOL, VIKINGS

The Vikings play in a **stadium** called the Metrodome. It is a special kind of building called a dome. Domes have round roofs. Vikings fans love watching games at the Metrodome. They sing a song called "Skol, Vikings" every time the Vikings score. *Skol* is an old Scandinavian word. It means "cheers." In the song, though, "skol, Vikings" means "way to go, Vikings."

Minnesota fans are famous for dressing up as Vikings from the old days. Some fans dress head-to-toe in purple! Vikings fans also call the team the Vikes and the Purple. The Vikings' biggest **rivals** are the Green Bay Packers and the Chicago Bears.

This fan is dressed as a Viking for a play-off game between the Vikings and the Philadephia Eagles. He even painted his face purple!

THEIR FIRST SUPER BOWL

There were **professional** football teams in Minnesota before the Vikings. None of them had much success, though. The Twin Cities needed a good team. The Vikings joined the NFL in 1960. In 1961, they played their first regular-season game. They beat the Chicago Bears!

Quarterback Fran Tarkenton scored five touchdowns in the Vikings' first game. He became one of the best NFL players of all time. Fans were sad when Minnesota traded Tarkenton to the New York Giants in 1967. However, the Vikings were a great team even without him. They reached the Super Bowl at the end of the 1969 season. They lost to the Kansas City Chiefs, though.

The Vikings played the Kansas City Chiefs in their first Super Bowl, on January 11, 1970. The Vikings lost the game, 23–7.

PURPLE PEOPLE EATERS

Minnesota came back from its Super Bowl loss and became one of the NFL's best teams in the 1970s. There was a popular song then called "The Purple People Eater." Fans called the 1970s team the Purple People Eaters because they were a tough team, and they wore purple uniforms.

The Giants traded Tarkenton back to Minnesota in 1973. The star quarterback led the Vikings to three Super Bowls in the 1970s. However, they lost those games to the Miami Dolphins, the Pittsburgh Steelers, and the Oakland Raiders. Even so, the Vikings set a record by becoming the first NFL team to play in four Super Bowls.

Strong defensive players such as Wally Hilgenberg (left) and Jim Marshall (center) helped the Vikings earn the nickname the Purple People Eaters.

A NEW HOME

The Vikings played in Metropolitan Stadium from their first season until the end of the 1981 season. By then, Metropolitan Stadium was getting old. The Vikings moved into their new stadium, the Metrodome, in 1982.

The Vikings continued to play well in the 1980s. They had great players like quarterback Tommy Kramer and **wide receiver** Anthony Carter. They were still a good team. They were not quite as good as they had been in the 1970s, though. The Vikings failed to reach a Super Bowl in the 1980s. They did make it to the **play-offs** five times, though. Only the best NFL teams even make it to the play-offs.

Vikings cornerback John Swain is shown intercepting a pass during a play-off game between the Vikings and the Washington Redskins in 1983.

STARS OF THE 1990S

The Vikings had been good in the 1980s. They became great again in the 1990s, though. The Vikings reached the play-offs seven times during that **decade**.

A wide receiver named Cris Carter joined the Vikings in 1990. Carter went on to break several team records. He was one of the best wide receivers who had ever played for the Vikings. Star quarterbacks Warren Moon and Randall Cunningham led the team in great games during the 1990s. A young wide receiver named Randy Moss joined the team in 1998 and quickly became a star. No team wanted to face the Vikings.

Wide receiver Cris Carter, shown here, broke many team records in the 12 seasons that he played for the Vikings.

THROWING AND RUNNING

In the early 2000s, Daunte Culpepper served as the Vikings' starting quarterback. Most quarterbacks score touchdowns by throwing the ball. Culpepper could also run to score touchdowns. In 2007, the Vikings **drafted** a **running back** named Adrian Peterson. It did not take Peterson long to become the best running back in the NFL.

Many people were surprised when quarterback Brett Favre joined the team in 2009. At first, Vikings fans did not like Favre because he had played for the Vikings' rival, the Packers. Soon they loved him! The Vikings once again had some of the best players in football.

Here, quarterback Brett Favre calls out a play to his teammates as the Vikings face the New Orleans Saints in 2010.

WINNING THAT SUPER BOWL

The Vikings seem to have bad luck when it comes to Super Bowls. They have won other big games over the years, though. The real Vikings from history were some of the most feared fighters who ever lived. The football Vikings are some of the most feared players in the NFL!

Other teams hate to play against Adrian Peterson. He is still one of the best running backs in the game. The Vikings also have a smart head **coach** named Brad Childress. Fans hope the Vikings have what it takes to win a Super Bowl for the Twin Cities at last!

In 2007, Vikings running back Adrian Peterson, shown here, broke the NFL record for most rushing yards in one game, with 296 yards.

MINNESOTA VIKINGS TIMELINE

1960

The Minnesota Vikings join the NFL.

1961

The Vikings play their first regular-season game. They beat the Chicago Bears, 37–13.

1967

The Vikings trade Fran Tarkenton to the New York Giants.

1970

The Vikings play in their first Super Bowl. They lose to the Kansas City Chiefs.

1977

The Vikings become the first NFL team to play in four Super Bowls.

1982

The Vikings beat the Tampa Bay Buccaneers in their first regular-season game in the Metrodome.

1998

The Vikings become the third team in the NFL to win 15 games in the regular season.

2006

Brad Childress becomes the head coach of the Vikings.

2007

The Vikings pick Adrian Peterson in the NFL draft.

GLOSSARY

COACH (KOHCH) A person who directs a team.

CONFERENCE (KON-feh-rents) A grouping of sports teams.

DECADE (DEH-kayd) A period of 10 years.

DRAFTED (DRAFT-ed) Picked to play on a professional sports team.

LEAGUE (LEEG) A group of sports teams.

LOGO (LOH-goh) A picture, words, or letters that stand for a team or company.

PLAY-OFFS (PLAY-ofs) Games played after the regular season ends to see who will play in the championship game.

PROFESSIONAL (pruh-FESH-nul) Having players who are paid.

QUARTERBACK (KWAHR-ter-bak) A football player who directs the team's plays.

RIVALS (RY-vulz) Two people or groups of people who try to get or to do the same thing as each other.

RUNNING BACK (RUN-ing BAK) A football player whose job is to take or catch the ball and run with it.

STADIUM (STAY-dee-um) A place where sports are played.

SUPER BOWLS (SOO-per BOHLZ) The championship games of NFL football.

WIDE RECEIVER (WYD rih-SEE-ver) A football player whose biggest job is to catch passes from the quarterback.

INDEX

WEB SITES

Due to the changing nature of Internet links, PowerKids Press has developed an online list of Web sites related to the subject of this book. This site is updated regularly. Please use this link to access the list:
www.powerkidslinks.com/teams/fvikings/